Chester the Chick

**For a free color catalog describing Gareth Stevens' list
of high-quality children's books call 1 (800) 433-0942**

Library of Congress Cataloging-in-Publication Data

Burton, Jane.
    Chester the chick / by Jane Burton; photography by Jane Burton
and Kim Taylor. — North American ed.
        p.   cm. — (Baby animals growing up)
    Includes index.
    Summary: Text and photographs follow a baby chick through its
first year of life as it learns how to peck for food, plays with other chicks, and
develops into a rooster.
    ISBN 0-8368-0204-7
    1. Chicks—Juvenile literature. 2. Chickens—Development—
Juvenile literature. [1. Chickens. 2. Animals—Infancy.]
I. Taylor, Kim, ill. II. Title. III. Series: Burton, Jane. Baby
animals growing up.
SF487.5.B87   1989
636.5'07—dc20   89-11421

This North American edition first published in 1989 by

Gareth Stevens Children's Books
7317 W. Green Tree Road
Milwaukee, Wisconsin 53223, USA

Format © 1989 by Gareth Stevens, Inc. Supplementary text © 1989 by
Gareth Stevens, Inc. Original text and photographs © 1988 by Jane Burton.
First published in Great Britain in 1988 by Macdonald & Co. Ltd.

Editors: Patricia Lantier and Rhoda Irene Sherwood
Cover design: Kate Kriege

Printed in the United States of America

1 2 3 4 5 6 7 8 9 95 94 93 92 91 90 89

Baby
Animals
Growing
Up!

Chester the Chick

JANE BURTON

Gareth Stevens Children's Books
MILWAUKEE

Sally Lightfoot's eggs are hatching! The first two chicks are already out and walking about, but she cannot leave the nest yet. She can hear the sounds of tapping and cheeping still going on underneath her.

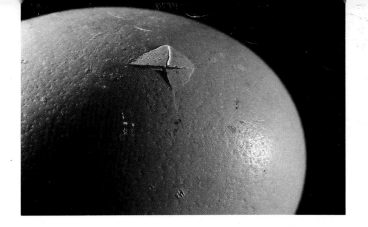

The last chick to hatch is Chester. He pushes up a small pip in the shell with his beak. He has a special egg tooth on the tip of his beak to help him hatch. He breaks away bits of shell until he has made a large hole. Then he rests.

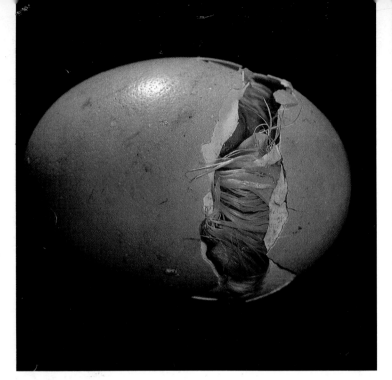 

Chester rests for a long time. When he is
ready, he goes to work again. Chester is
curled up tight inside his shell, with almost
no room to move. Yet he manages to turn
himself, little by little, by pushing with his
feet and elbowing with his wings. Each time
he turns, his beak taps out another bit of
shell. Turning and tapping, he quickly cuts
off the top of the egg.

Now only a hinge of skin holds the two halves
of the egg together. Heaving and pushing,
Chester tries to straighten his neck.
Suddenly he uncurls. The top of the shell
flies open like a lid of a box! Chester bursts
out, upside down. Quickly he scrambles the
right way up. Now he must rest again, while
his downy feathers dry and his legs get
strong. An hour later, half-dry, he can sit up.

8

One day old

Chester's down is dry and fluffy. He can stand up and run about. He still has the egg tooth on the tip of his beak, but he does not need it now. Soon it will drop off.

Sally Lightfoot is brooding her chicks. Chester pushes up among her feathers. Baby chicks need their mother to keep them warm. They cannot keep themselves warm until their feathers have grown. Beneath their mother, the chicks keep snug and dry.

Two days old

The next day Sally Lightfoot gets off her nest, leaving the empty shells behind. The chicks follow her closely. Because the chicks are still very tiny, she does not go far. She lies down to bask in the bright spring sunshine. The chicks stay close around her, pecking at this and that.

While Sally Lightfoot preens her feathers, the chicks look for things to eat. Baby chicks are born knowing how to peck up food. They peck at anything small, round, and shiny. Seeds and insects are good! Chester pecks at Sally Lightfoot's wattles while she is having a dust bath.

Three days old

Sally Lightfoot helps her chicks to find food. Picking up a crumb in her beak, she jerks her head up and down and clucks a special call that means food. The chicks rush and cluster around her head. One pecks the crumb from her beak, and the others peck from the ground where she is pointing. Small yellow petals look tasty and are worth trying.

The chicks are thirsty after eating dry crumbs. Chicks discover water in the same way they find food, by pecking at something shiny. Chester and his brothers peck at the shine around the rim of the water bowl. Each sips one mouthful at a time then, beak in the air, lets the drop trickle down his throat before taking another sip. This is how most birds drink.

While Chester has a little drink at the puddle, a large brown rat waddles over. The rat is thirsty and wants a drink too. But Sally Lightfoot gives a shriek of alarm. She jabs at the rat with her beak! Her chicks run to hide beneath her. The rat runs away.

Four days old

Chester wanders across the yard in the bright warm sunshine. Suddenly a cloud blots out the sun. A chill wind blows. Chester feels cold and lost.

A lost chick will stand and cry for help. Chester shouts "CHEEP! CHEEP! CHEEP!" His voice carries a very long way. Sally Lightfoot hears him and runs to rescue him. The relieved Chester creeps in among her feathers and is soon warm again.

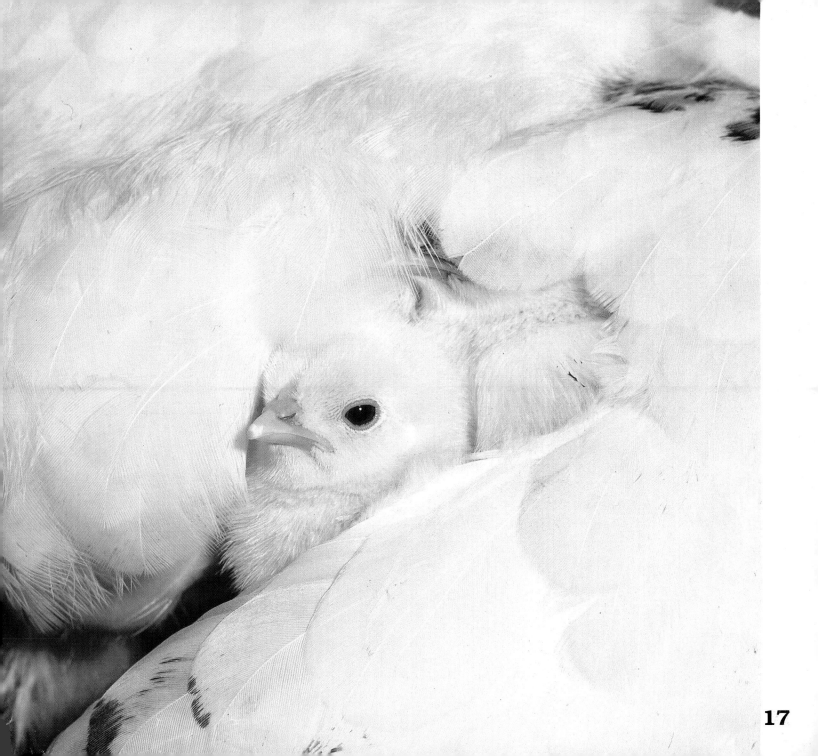

One week old

Chester and his brothers and sisters are already sprouting tiny wing feathers. The chicks are big enough to run all over the place, and they scratch about among the primroses. But they still stay near their mother. They rely on her for food and protection. If Sally Lightfoot finds a juicy insect, she does not eat it herself, but calls the chicks. Often Chester wins the race to grab the grub, but he has to run away fast with it or someone will snatch it from him.

But if Sally Lightfoot finds a bug that tastes nasty, she squawks "Yuk," warning the chicks not to touch it. She is always on the lookout for danger. If she spots a hawk flying over, she gives a warning call that tells the chicks "Hide!" The chicks dive for cover and lie low until Sally Lightfoot calls them out again when the danger has passed.

Three weeks old

When Chester is about three weeks old, his comb starts to show. He is so pale now that he is almost white, except on his face.

Four weeks old

Their wing feathers are growing well but the chicks still need their mother's warmth. Sally Lightfoot spreads herself so her brood can nestle among her feathers.

Five weeks old

Chester's wattles are growing, as well as his comb, but his sister has neither wattles nor comb yet. They are no longer pretty yellow chicks. Chester has grown into a leggy young cockerel, while Maggie is now a neat pullet.

Three to six months old

When the sun shines through them, Chester's comb and wattles glow bright red. White body plumage sprouts through his down. Chester's eye is as keen as a hawk's. He struts about and tries to crow, but all he can manage is a drawn-out squeak! Like tiny fighting cocks, he and his brothers strike at each other with their feet as they flutter and jump playfully together.

All the young cockerels are white with black speckles, and all the pullets are golden. The family stays together throughout summer. The sun has parched the grass, which is full of seed. Insects are everywhere. But soon it will be winter. When the trees lose their leaves, the birds will roost in the hen house instead of on a cold, bare branch.

23

Nine months to one year old

Winter has come. Chester and his brothers
are fully grown, with big, bright red combs
and glossy plumage. Today they are not very
happy. A biting cold wind blows over the
land. Scratching in the snow for corn, they
huddle to try to keep warm.

In the early spring one of Chester's sisters
begins to lay eggs. When the spring flowers
are out once again, her chicks have hatched.
Maggie is a good broody hen and has her
own special chicks to look after.

While the hens sit on their eggs or mind their chicks, Chester and his brothers keep watch. High on the wall they strut. Chester crows, with a loud ringing call — "Cock-a-doodle-doo!" His brothers crow too, each calling in turn. The cheerful sounds proclaim to other birds, "Keep out! All is well."

Fun Facts About Baby Chicks and Chickens

1. By watching their parents, baby chicks learn to scratch in the soil for food. But if they are fed by people who raise them, they can feed on mash — a finely ground blend of corn, wheat, oats, alfalfa, scraps of fish, and cod liver oil.

2. By taking a dust bath, chickens are able to keep themselves clean and free of pesky insects.

3. Thousands of years ago, wild birds that resembled chickens lived in the jungles of Asia. These birds roamed freely over the land until people captured them and raised them for food. The birds eventually became tame and were called chickens. They belong to the scientific family *Gallus*.

4. Eggshells can vary in color from white to brown to green, and may be solid or spotted. Color is determined by the ancestors of the chicken.

5. The language of chickens may be more varied than that of any other bird. For example, some chicken sounds are the crow, cackle, squeak, scream, squawk, chirp, chirr, peep, croak, sob, and song.

6. There are many superstitions about chickens. For example
    a. to see two chickens with their heads together as though they are talking is a sure sign that people are talking about you.
    b. when chickens' feathers droop, it is supposed to be a sure sign of rain.

7. In ancient Greece, fever, dysentery, melancholy, epilepsy, cough, and colic were all treated by application of various parts of the chicken. Oil of chicken eggs was guaranteed to make hair grow.

8. Warm chicken broth is still suggested today as a comforting, curing drink for anyone with a cold.

For More Information About Animal Life

Listed below are some books, magazines, and videocassettes that contain interesting facts about chickens. Check your local library or bookstore to see if they are there or if someone there can order them for you.

Books
The Beautiful Chick. Rausiri (Cellar)
A Chick Hatches. Cole (Morrow)
Cosmic Chickens. Delaney (Harper & Row Jr.)
Jessie the Chicken. Pursell (Carolrhoda Books)
Little Chicken. Brown (Harper & Row Jr.)
Little Chick's Story. Kwitz (Harper & Row Jr.)
The Little Red Hen. Berg (Modern Curriculum)
The Runaway Chick. Ravilious (Macmillan)
Sherlock Chick and the Peekaboo Mystery. Quackenbush (Parents)
The World of Chickens. Coldrey (Gareth Stevens)

Magazines
Chickadee
Young Naturalist Foundation
P.O. Box 11314
Des Moines, IA 50340

Owl
Young Naturalist Foundation
P.O. Box 11314
Des Moines, IA 50340

National Geographic World
National Geographic Society
P.O. Box 2330
Washington, DC 20013-9865

Ranger Rick
National Wildlife Federation
8925 Leesburg Pike
Vienna, VA 22184-0001

Videocassettes
Chick Chick Chick. Churchill Films, 1975.
The Chicken. Barr Films, 1986.

Things to Do

1. Try to arrange a trip to a chicken farm with a parent or teacher. Observe the behavior of the little chicks. See if they peck for food, and listen to the sounds they make. Try to notice how a mother hen will "brood" her chicks. See if you can feed the chicks some grain.

2. Some children get little chicks as pets at Easter. Sometimes these chicks are a different color than yellow! Find out how chicks can be dyed. Try to find out if this is really a safe procedure.

3. Go to the library and look at an encyclopedia or pictures of chickens in animal books. Are there many types? Decide on three of your favorite types and write a paragraph on each, describing their appearance and interesting habits.

4. Draw and color the three main stages of the growing process of a male chicken: (1) the baby chick; (2) the young cockerel; and (3) the rooster. When you have finished the drawings, give a special name to your young rooster.

5. Find out what "cockfighting" is. Do you think this is a good idea for a sport? Why or why not? Should this be a legal activity? Why or why not?

Things to Talk About

1. Sally Lightfoot "broods" her chicks. This means that she keeps them warm by surrounding them underneath her body feathers. How do others help to keep you warm when you are cold?

2. Baby chicks are born knowing how to peck food from the ground for themselves. Some of the things they try to eat are good, and some are not. How does this compare with children when they are allowed to choose their own food?

3. When Chester is lost, he stands still and cries for help until his mother comes. Have you ever been lost before, for example, in a department store or at a carnival? What did you do? Discuss some possible ways to get help if you accidentally get lost.

4. Chester and his brothers help to protect their families as they grow older. Does this seem familiar to the way men you know act toward their families? What are some of the ways men protect their loved ones?

5. As Chester grows, his voice changes! For a long time, all he can do is squeak; after a long time, he is finally able to crow. How is this process similar to the one that happens to young humans as they become teenagers? Explain why you think this happens.

6. Does the behavior of the chicks toward their mothers change as they get older? If so, in what ways? Does this seem like a normal process to you? Explain.

7. Discuss what the idea of "family loyalty" means. Do Chester and his family show loyalty to each other? When is this an important part of family life?

Glossary of New Words

bask: to sunbathe; to warm up by staying out in the sun

beak: a bird's bill

brood: to sit on and hatch eggs; it also refers to all the baby animals in a family

cockerel: a young rooster, less than a year old

comb: a red, fleshy growth on the top of the head, as on a rooster

down: the soft, fine feathers of young birds

grub: the short, fat, wormlike larva of an insect

hatch: the successful effort of a baby animal to leave its egg

hen: the female chicken

jab: to poke or punch in a quick manner

nestle: to settle down closely and snugly

peck: to pick up objects and food with the beak

plumage: the feathers of a bird

preen: in relation to birds, to clean and trim the feathers with the beak

pullet: a young hen, not more than a year old

scramble: to climb, scuffle, or struggle quickly for something

shriek: to scream; to make a loud, piercing cry

snatch: to grab or seize quickly or suddenly

wattles: a fleshy, wrinkled, colorful piece of skin that hangs from the chin or throat of some birds

31

Index

636.5   Burton, Jane
BuR
         Chester the chick

DATE DUE

APR 4	JUN 0	OCT 1 8	JAN 2 1
MAY 12	OCT 2 2	DEC 1 4	FEB 2 4
MAY 15	NOV 2 3	JAN 7	APR 5
OCT 14	DEC 0 9	FEB 9 -	
NOV	JAN 2 0	MAR 3 -	
NOV 21	FEB 8	MAR 2 5	
FEB 09	Mar. 19	MAY 04	
FEB 26	MAR 2 2	DEC 0 5	
MAR 23	APR 1 3	JAN 0 8	